Controlled Hallucinations

John Sibley Williams

FUTURECYCLE PRESS
www.futurecycle.org

Copyright © 2013 John Sibley Williams
All Rights Reserved

Published by FutureCycle Press
Hayesville, North Carolina, USA

ISBN 978-1-938853-22-7

Contents

I.	11
II.	12
III.	13
IV.	14
V.	15
VI.	16
VII.	17
VIII.	18
IX.	19
X.	20
XI.	21
XII.	22
XIII.	23
XIV.	24
XV.	25
XVI.	26
XVII.	27
XVIII.	28
XIX.	29
XX.	30
XXI.	31
XXII.	32
XXIII.	33
XXIV.	34
XXV.	35
XXVI.	36
XXVII.	37
XXVIII.	38
XXIX.	39
XXX.	40
XXXI.	41
XXXII.	42
XXXIII.	43
XXXIV.	44
XXXV.	45

XXXVI	46
XXXVII	47
XXXVIII	48
XXXIX	49
XL	50
XLI	51
XLII	52
XLIII	53
XLIV	54
XLV	55
XLVI	56
XLVII	57
XLVIII	58
XLIX	59
L	60
LI	61
LII	62
LIII	63
LIV	64
LV	65
LVI	66
LVII	67
LVIII	68
LIX	69
LX	70
LXI	71
LXII	72
LXIII	73

to the coming extinctions

6.

To be the ideal obsession
        itself—
neither dreamer nor the dreamt but
        the dream,
the slow song left uncomposed
between morning eye
and morning bird.
To be their conversation.

To be neither ocean
nor another drop that falls into it
but what it means to rise
        together
        just an inch.

To be the effect.
To be a thoughtful pause
and restrained response.
To be the passion of raking nails.
To be taste, any taste.
To be the concept behind
an unpainted mural.
To be ink. To be color.
To be the scent
translated as toxin
or perfume,
        depending.
To be the heart when a gaze sweeps inward
        or out.
To be the seeds planted by progress.
To be the seeds planted by regression.
To be astonishment.

To be love
        itself,
neither the loving
nor the beloved.
To be translatable.

To be chalked up to experience.
To be experience.
To be the waking
each morning
without having to wake.

To be, just once,
an unending conversation.

Controlled Hallucinations

I.

I see a man on an adjacent building,
silhouette cut from the skyline.
So I also cut out the roof
he stands on.
I cut out the tools
and the cascading shingles.
I cut out the hydrangeas
the shingles decapitate
on their way down.

I cut out the mountain
in the distance,
still coddling its last snows,
replacing it with a silo,
the shingles with paper
snowflakes.

I replace the man
with another man
with a woman
with a horse
a piano
with a book
and myself.

Nothing quite fits.

But the man
no longer fits either
or the roof
or skyline.
And I wonder is this
what it means
to touch?

II.

Buda pest.

Two unique names converge.

From their vantage points
on opposing sides of a river,
which is yielding more
to bear this simplicity of shape,
this married language?

Surely, it must be the other
leaning into deformity.
Always it must be the other.

Either way, the maps need changing.

Names are no longer irreducible
to themselves.

III.

In a country where everyone is mute,
I'm throwing my body into a silent dance
without a single voice to complain
while strumming my fingers along the many
closed worlds of language.

What is the sound of a shared idea?
What is the sound of your agreement?

IV.

There's no pattern to our astonishment.

Birds don't know
the weight placed on them.
They look down and see
us looking up.

That is all it takes
when there is no gravity
but flight

and falling.

But not falling exactly—
no separation moment:
love from body,
experience from its magnitude,
thought from love of itself.

How long the ripples echo
from the stones and prayers
skipped across the sky,
how far the crumbs must fall
from our hands
to be evenly dispersed.

Pockets heavied by stones
and falling,
I await a less scattered return
of all I've flung
as far as astonishment would allow
and all I've dropped, unnoticed,
upon the surface.

V.

She calls me to the window.
With the current of winter frost
breath struggles to converse.
Against the current of conversation
a relentless, accurate darkness.

I know the bottom well,
she claims.
And the tender views it affords.

Outside the night dances its silence.
She calls me to our window
and points to a ship
upon the near-distant river,
mast lit by thousands of bulbs
I cannot see.

VI.

Let's use the abandoned factory,
the one our children first spoke of
in ghosts and shadows
and now as safe haven for all
we cannot accept at home.

Let's tear at each other
like strangers,
screaming out forgotten names
without offending,
sighing every name
except each other's.

Let's leave our clothes
where salmon was gutted—
socks dangling like entrails
from the hooks and bricks,
underwear pooled
in the gathering rust.

Let's forget, for a moment,

and return, naked, exhausted,
to the now fishless river

and try to swim upstream.

VII.

At a certain distance
the flower's withering
is beautiful
and the river
I've chosen to cross
seems purposeful
and the page
upon which I've been written
turns sideways—
landscape to portrait.

And though looking into these mirrors
I've placed in things
is strange,
stranger still
the cold fact of photographs
and perspective—
what really changes
when a head turns sideways
and taste is exposed
as preference.

This river I've accepted as mine is the choice
between these most intimate cannibalisms.

VIII.

Night does not arrive
or roll in
or whisper
or shriek its presence.

If the air troubled with mystery,
      perhaps.
If it struggled between
barraging us with silence
and barraging us with fact
and then left more
than what it stole.
If it truly stole
or endowed us with breath.
If every room
had a wide-open window
with ocean views,
      perhaps

it would matter
how we articulate
the disappearance of light.

IX.

Inseparable: the growing
and the plastic flowers,
the face, its mirror,
the roots lost deep below the surface
and the few that break through.

When does it end,
this search for a more intimate gravity,
this need to replicate embrace?

The paper cut on my palm
runs parallel to my love line.
They taper off at the same spot,
under my thumb.

I'm writing ecstatically
about the simple perfection
of your sleeping figure

from another room.

X.

I carve up my mother
with the delicate edges of leaves,
my father with stubborn pine needles,
my dead grandparents with their own weather,
my devoted wife with moss,

then chew them slowly
in that order
every morning.

With nothing left
weighted to my life,
I cut tomorrow into flavorless little chunks,
stacking the bones I can't digest
into a fragile structure
so my child will learn something of home,
so this child in my hands
learns early how to swallow.

XI.

We are born of a question
and dance together
    apart
    together
as its answer.

We are born and rush from
the dim room of certainties
    out
into the vast, bright
    unanswerable.

You are born and I am born
    every day
    as strangers.

The wonder isn't that we love
as if from different cities
but that we are different cities
    absent railroad tracks, wires, common language,
yet still we wake
    in unison.

XII.

I would like to crochet a mitten
for my future child,
      to warm another's hands
      with the work of my own.

I would like to build a house for someone,
      anyone,
      a stranger,
      from foundation to wafting chimney,
and then smile at the pain
of pressing on the bruises
left from making.

But all I have is a song to lean on,
      an eager voice,
      a white cane
      related to me as stone is to moss,
and I am hoping
this simple attempt at light will suffice.

XIII.

My heart is a hammer.
With it I fix the house
I pried apart
just moments ago

and will again
raze and rebuild
tomorrow.

My house is a heart
with too many chambers,
too many purposes,
too many rhythms.

Blood hurries through me
without sanctuary,
without nourishment,
without looking back.

XIV.

These hastily made masks,
so ornate, so colorful—
stoic and utterly
broken,

no two alike—

the bus overflows
the city overflows
the country overflows
with slipped-on portraits
to hide the one face
we refuse to share.

XV.

The entirety of human history
is scrawled in graffiti
on a single gray brick
trying to loosen itself
from the red wall.

Can you hear its tender body
screaming its uniqueness,
screaming its name, screaming
and settling
for a heaven to scale?

Soon I'll know what that feels like—

my fingers losing their gray
with each honest touch,
my nameless mouth screaming
louder and louder
with each inescapable act of unity.

XVI.

Just moments before the rest of the world,

I drive my last fencepost into the hard earth
and take a handful of birds from the sky
and release them back
        only partially changed.

In conversing with the older forests,
I implore their trees for sturdier roots.
I follow the parallel lines
to that time and place where they touch,

    where, invisible and underground, I am the roots
and their groans from continually stretching out
        and up,
where I am part of the rest of the world
and can rain invisible
over my miles of rotted fenceposts
and my muddy field.

XVII.

The coin in my hand is good,
but I'm unable to board.
The doors are open,
steps drawn down to the pavement—
    no bar blocking my way,
    no driver.

The bus crawling so slowly
I could accidentally fall into it,
    both
hungry and sated,
waiting for movement
and already moving.

Don't look up, don't look up.
What if the seats are all empty
and still I cannot sit?

What if they are all empty
after I occupy them?

XVIII.

Forks   knives   spoons.

A well-lit room
with too many clocks.

The coins saved
from forgetting
each toll.

All these burnt offerings
uncollected
by static deities.

And the mirrors, always
the fractured bits of myself
screaming from within
whatever I try to touch.

I lay them carefully
around my heart.

I whisper them into
the deep well out back.

I plant them
like wheat in the ocean,
like salmon eggs in a cornfield,

and bind the rest of me
to their tiny
tiny anchor.

XIX.

In the middle of the bridge, where
I cannot put my back to the world.

In the middle of the bridge, where
any step crosses a threshold,
    so I do not step.

In the middle of the bridge, where
I can safely contemplate
these lesser drownings
    and my part in them.

In the middle of the river, floating
on my back, bloated
from too many drinks
of memory,
looking up at the sturdy iron bridge,
    each of us raw on one side.

XX.

The sky of this poem
is not *that* sky.
Wind drives words
from the thousand and one
ongoing conversations,
        disbanding and re-
        joining, each plea
        a whole new
        life—

another sign of restoration,
another white-knuckled prayer,
another ode dedicated
to the coming extinctions—

a hollow shell capturing
a single sound
that, pressed to ear,
echoes every other,

like when in loud voices stars emerge
all around us,
        silently.

XXI.

When I was a child
and a storm approached,
>others assisted their families
>with the shutters and shovels,
>others counted the time between
>claps and flashes—

I would cry out a list of synonyms
for what was to come:

>*tempest blizzard gale squall cloudburst*
>*chaos*
>*upheaval*

(We were then what we would soon become.)

I still react in words, take comfort in their distance.

XXII.

The very birds are mute.

Their anxious trees are talking.

> The rusty sky is moving, jaded
> and alone, across our quieting demands.

But voices will emerge again, some day.

There is still much to pretend to work toward.

> This would be easier to witness in winter.

XXIII.

I scrutinize the rain
paused over our bed
and look to you
for an answer.
.

How to know if this
is the water hour,
if the path has forked,
if the arc is concave?
.

You're still sleeping
somewhere outside me.
.

Should I fetch the umbrella?
Should I wake you
from these dreams
of others
and ask?
.

I am naked
but for a T-shirt
and the choices I've made.

XXIV.

Perhaps this is the chance
to undefine
the laws of gravity
that have struggled
against
our rediscovering play.

The air in our lungs
is voiceless
but not silent.
Our voices are drained
to near full.

We are ready.

Let's open with a
simpler song
this time,
one borrowed
from our archives
of unashamed
nakedness,

and climb through
each other
like windows
unmolested by their grand views.

XXV.

Soaked to bone by the world—
behind each step glistens
a shallow heart-puddle
that speaks only in reversals,
aftermaths, and other tricks of light,

in turns, all at the same time—

a welcome distraction
for grounding all these confident
songs of destination.

XXVI.

Description of the sky,
the reds and blues that embrace
whatever mood we offer them—
> starry eruptions,
> bizarre translucents,
> variations on the shared
> themes of solitude

> or of conversation.

Weather is a choice.

And maybe hands are this too.

Maybe the old stones of libraries
are plastic building blocks
stacked, knocked down, rebuilt
with each new experience,

Maybe the song of footsteps
metered into hardwood stairs
is a kind of knocking.

Maybe the reflection
of one building in another
is my face.

I choose another color
and, now, that
> is sky.

I stroke the farthest edge of love
and unfind my silence.

With ease, I enter into all things
> and dissolve.

XXVII.

Consider the sea a skewed mirror
and churning your uncertain limbs through its waves
an attempt to untangle light.

The comforting density of bone and future
mean little here.
The world is too light
to trouble with tomorrow,
too buoyant to sink with you.

So bring the background forward.
Kick up ripples and silt through that secret face.
Distort it into accuracy.

Where your faces finally meet
you will float without need for movement,
as in the Dead Sea
but without the need for salt.
Water can be your single taut thread—
      reflecting.

Later there will be plenty of time
to learn to walk.

XXVIII.

> "I was like a tunnel. Birds fled from me."
> —*Pablo Neruda*

In these small, broken lines
a thirst for order,
a gathering of original elements,
a house of words to hold them,

a kind of following—
      the bird ahead of me moves left
      then I move left
      then down—

and a hope
that all flight is logical
      and safe,
even without fixed destination.

Even without your small, broken kiss
I am like a tunnel
confined by light.

XXIX.

Don't be late!

In half an hour
we'll be casting
our permanent roles
in each other's lives.

XXX.

I fell into the Grand Canyon and broke
the rose in my eye
that I'd carefully planned to see through
when encountering such obvious
        illumination.

XXXI.

Hurry, symptom.

Hurry, doctor.

Hurry first incision,
    dull blade,
        and the sharper pain
        of needle and thread.

.

The universe was written
in the form of a question

that has straightened
and walks differently now.

.

Hurry, light
    (amazed and agonized light).
Lay down your luminescence.

My spine is tired of knowing itself.

XXXII.

Innumerable photographs
spread across the bed—
in long-dead monochrome,
in overexposed daylight,

so many unique deformities
alongside overused tropes
the eye passes over,

so many unstoppable firestorms
grown cold,
so many safe images of home
burning long into sleep.

In time, everything has become
unforgettable
and forgotten.
.

The windows are shut tight,
the room unmoved,
yet still I must stack
something heavier upon the past
so it doesn't blow away.

XXXIII.

    Gone
the perfection that was never quite perfect.

Gone the edgeless sea,
       uncompromised dreams,
       mother's arms.

Gone this dull blade of expectation,
       this tremor lodged
       in the glassed-in heart,
       always looking out
       through half-beats.

The horizon is swept away,
leaving only my hands
and what they can touch.

The piano in the corner bares its teeth,
       each note incomplete—
       never to run its course.

I devour the note,
shatter the heart,
become that tender outline of
       just enough.

XXXIV.

We've lost the school beneath the mango tree.
.

Words for taste drip down my chin—
    I must speak *saccharine*
    to know they are sweet.
.

Her sex uproots, climbs from the bed
to stand on my eyelids—
    I'm developing a thesis on conversation.
.

We've lost the sun and shade and a belief
in bodies—
    I'm reeducating myself in hope.
.

This is a song
    I must repeat
        down into my bones.

XXXV.

I dimly remember
      being
      water
running from the gables.

I am sorry
but

the leaves
      were on fire.
Their trees
      on fire.
The grass
and, within,
our buried toes
      on fire.

I am sorry
but

all summer
they had pleaded
for rain
      together
      in one voice,

and my open hands
come with a flood of caveats.

XXXVI.

A nightingale speaks to its reflection in the window
though it seems to be advising us on important matters.

Nobody taught me conversation either.

When out in the garden, I plant only the heartiest fruits,
those guaranteed to become food.
I must know what's under each stone before I look.

This, my love, is why I approach you sideways,
why I let this body articulate a deeper silence,
why my lips freeze around the vowels in your name.

It's why this poem is not for you,
why I've pulled down the mirrors,
why the walls are white squares of dust
framing empty metal hooks.

The window watches both directions, intently,
though only one at a time.

There is everything left to discuss.

This is no nightingale.

XXXVII.

The air is saccharine.
The wind is saccharine.
Our breath is saccharine,

    leaving behind a trail of broken things.

XXXVIII.

Through the lackluster light
a bird
the size of sixty birds
blackly
descends
on my laundry line

and begins to feast
on the bird
the size of no true bird
that I'd just drawn
for you
from distant memory

on this

forgotten

anniversary.

XXXIX.

    Do not worry.
The knives I display in this poem
cannot even cut an overripe fruit.

When I thrash them wildly
or hold them to your throat, or mine,
when I threaten an old enemy
with a few unsharpened words
or dismember my own truths
slice by slice,
      just know
I only wish for the air around us to bleed.

XL.

      Love,
this mess is a conscious effort,
an experiment on hunger,
on what happens
when a single loaf is placed
in my hands.

Thank you for the bread.

Thank you for neglecting to sweeten it.

And thank you for leaving
the crumbs where they lie

upon the mantle and doorframe,
scattered across the bed sheets
and page,
so they can harvest themselves.

And thank you for licking my fingers clean
so I can forget I am full.

XLI.

Maintain the weightlessness of hummingbird flight.
Maintain the weightlessness of grammar.
Hook parentheses around the mantras
I try to chant into existence
      (setting them apart from other birds).
Force quotation marks around the experiences
I hope never to forget.

Strike out the failures I jealously guard,
then strike out the triumphs
      (to maintain balance).

Maintain the weightlessness of font.
Change it as easily as wings change destination.
Misplace a dash
or the white space around it
and feel the epiphany quake, alter—

feel meaning fall into its own gravity.

XLII.

Most of me
attended
the Big Bang
just to ask it
if other theories
were possible.

My feet
paced holes
in the cosmos,
waiting.

My mouth
prepared
to endlessly
repeat
the appraisal.

My heart quivered.
My heart started
and stopped
quivering.

It answered.

I'd left
my ears
far below
on your
sleeping chest.

XLIII.

Immersed in the game,
our shadow puppets
are devouring the rest of the bedroom wall,
are nesting upon the ceiling and door frames
      where we cannot follow.

.

Everything is food for creation.

Everything began with us
shaping white mountains from gray pillows,
shaping silhouettes from our lovemaking.

Everything has grown hungry
for more of itself.

.

Our hands are the same size.

XLIV.

While the photographer develops his film
and the throes of ordinary life resume,
I am left to pose alone—

someone else's leg draped over my ritual chair,
a new suit I didn't buy,
this knitted brow of knowing
eternity is static
and feigning my indifference.

Chemicals are blending in the next room.
I can smell what it means
to no longer be temporary.
I'm reliving a certain schoolboy violence,
leaving it nearer the surface.

Not enough has been taken from me.

My face is still turned to the window
as it will be in the picture.
I can't see out either glass.

Heavy light eclipses one half of one eye,
as if I'm analyzing the tooth marks
left on a mirror.

XLV.

Let's be moths together
circling the bright eye,
circling and trying to enter,
then retreating as far as darkness allows.

No movement is futile.

Once we've burned through the candles
and burned through the moon,
let's think bigger—
let's be birds
circling the morning sun
with only brief tree shade for respite.

But let's stay far from the trees;
let's be fully lit,
to whatever consequence.

Let's be birds together for a moment,
hollering across this shared distance,
and see if the sky is too small.

XLVI.

Always too late for unmaking,
an image passes through my eye,

writhing in memory's digestion,
conforming its shape to temporary norms.

With it the whole body shivers.

Skin is also a photograph.

And this photo unravels
in the story of older light-shapes,
when grass colored differently
and clouds did not rush
from the frame.

If the eye is a series of rooms
with changing dimensions,
how to tell if this is still the bedroom—
the walls repainted,
that reliable rectangle of sky
now a circle,
the fixed image just captured
unable to settle on its film.

XLVII.

The artists have brought
all their incidental colors
to bear
this empty coffin—
      riding low on our shoulders—
to a deeper surface.

They've carved a perfect
representation of
      "Human Body: Alive"
on the stark ivory lid.

I sign my name
in another's blood.

We're masters at faking
      failure
and contrasting

what has always been
      against
its own static background.

XLVIII.

Forks and knives dull,
teeth worn down,
I am left to eat
in broken English.

I try to step around the flavors
passed through so many mouths,
around the stacks
of overused plates
that have cracked
with wear—
      the only plates at the table.
I try to trace each cliché back
to a curious hand
tapping a white cane
in hopes of rediscovering
my blindness.

XLIX.

I am most defined by this hatred of fire escapes
and the concession of sorting waves by their direction.

Nobody leaves the night in pieces anymore.

Why not strike out for all shores at once
with the honest ferocity of *attempt*
and climb from amnesia
wearing only socks, carrying a net?

I concede there is no true nudity left.
I make love dressed in all the world's lovemaking.
The pieces of other bodies combine perfectly
into my outline.

So I try to climb as far from myself as stairs allow.
I'm huffing by the third floor.
The railings are rusted. It's always raining.
And the roof will only be so high.

L.

A blackened ball of yarn
     jerking,
          tugging free of itself,
unwinding between two
curious orange paws—

that's how it moves,

this steady
inconsistent
eternity.

LI.

Naked of metaphor,
a cell stands alone
within the ecstatic movement of blood.

No longer a simple parable
aggrandizing the utter chaos
and epiphany of smaller change—
that obsession of waking
to find your life too vast to measure.

Blood speaks the made-up language of truth.
I cannot pretend to be deaf.

I am no transient here.

LII.

To stand
in the static center of a fan
long enough,
lighter particles
      whipping their never-
      ending circles
will begin to see you
as movement,
themselves as inert.
.

When I close one eye,
the other tries to compensate
and you become the background
in my photograph.

LIII.

The shutter clicks.

.

Our love is now timeless.

LIV.

Each morning the clock mislays one second
and another as I wind back its hand.
The sunlight upon its face
is beginning again
to haul timber from the deep forest.
I am wearing its undress.

Of all sinking things,
only this moment will be saved—
my fingers choked back in my mouth
and the song of an old brass instrument
over empty seats.

LV.

We silently walk the alleys
that cut deep into cold
blocks of architecture
while rubbing each other
with these phantom limbs
that still tingle,
still reach bitterly
for substance,

still reach,

finding animal warmth
and semi-permanence
in their unbroken dreams
of building up
and pulling toward
a shared conversation
that will never cease.

LVI.

To bear the seeds
To bear the seeds of a small-scale hell
To bear the seeds of a small-scale hell
slowly extinguishing into that long-sought
patiently awaited   nondescript

        epiphany—

    something about cloud shapes and childhood,
    a windless curtain dancing, a toppled candle, all vaguely
    the color white.

LVII.

Each lake is a pinhole
poked from a larger map of land.

Each nameless roadside creek
is born of curious scissors.

I am sorry,
cartographer of my life.

I love the water too much
to stop drilling here.

LVIII.

Normally of fixed arrows,
the bird flight today is   splintered wood
from a dislodged tree—

like tiny backlit silhouettes
floating upon the arguing blue currents,
     together and apart
and together.

The wood shows signs of recent fire.

There has not been a storm here in some time.

LIX.

With an apple in my mouth, yes,
I must be swine.
Because strangers stop momentarily
to capture me in their lenses,
I must be a roadside attraction.
As there is nothing to hold to
in what I say,
>   I say it again
>   and again—

nonsense being the tenderest
act of friendship, of identity.

I can be cloudburst, yes,
and I can be my own prey.
I can be you
>   or, if you say it,
>   none of these.

LX.

I shall wear the afternoon sun
rolling through autumn leaves like water
when it suits my purpose.
Sometimes, however,
the strange eroticism of Greek statues,
limbs cleaved and missing,
or the myth of winged cherubs.

On those days I will be stone
and history's masturbation.
I will leave nothing to its own forgetting.

When a tear provokes me to hope,
and for a moment I am less of the past,
I as seed will be planted
in neat, consecutive rows
across a most fertile basin,
unfurling through season after season
a plan impossible to sow.

LXI.

Each house is built on a hill
sloping toward a growling unseen river,
ascending toward the lowest-reaching clouds.

Surrounding the house, high walls
scrawled in half-songs,
each composed in another's blood,
and half-dreams
and other unrecognizable things.

Which view have you chosen
for the bedroom?
Which gravity will you follow?

LXII.

I have been marked:
    a poet,

    not a fisherman,
    cobbler,
    or soldier.

Nothing is less important

yet words fall from our mouths,
assuming identity,
imbuing meaning,
clouding the white space.

Let me go into this void.
    Lose me there
where fish may hook themselves,
where language hauls away its spoils
leaving crisp, colorless oblivion—

Tomorrow you may remember me as
    a silent musician
    or a flightless bird;
    as a dead horse,
    a poet,
    or a deep shadow, fulfilled.

LXIII.

The rough edges of a church's cornerstone
or the guilty side
of a prison wall
or the innocent.

This tree might one day be
a hearth's fire
or a cross
looming high over
abandoned winter fields.

Either the house is being torn down
around us
or our feet
are permanent.

As it should be.

Look up to discover
a tiny tear in the cold blue curtain
and struggle the rest of your life
not to pull down the sky.
.

I know only one thing:
there is no un-
knowing.

Acknowledgments

Special thanks to A. Molotkov for his detailed review and suggestions and to Mark S. R. Struzan and the rest of the Moonlit Poetry team for their critiques.

And, as always, to Staci M. Williams for her inspiration and support.

The author sends his heartfelt gratitude to the following journals for publishing poems in *Controlled Hallucinations*: *322 Review, Atticus Review, Barnwood International, Blue Five Notebook, Blue Lake Review, Calliope Nerve, The Copperfield Review, Counterexample Poetics, Five Poetry Journal, IMPROV 2011 Anthology, M Review, Missive, Moon Milk Review, The Neglected Ratio, Other Rooms, Pipe Dream, Poetic Matrix, Poets and Artists, Red Ochre Lit, Scythe Literary Journal, Small Doggies, Spork Press, Subliminal Interiors, Sugar House Review, Symmetry Pebbles, Toe Good, The Tower Journal, The Unrorean,* and *Unshod Quills.*

And to *The Pinch Literary Journal,* for selecting "Description of the Sky" as 2nd place winner for their 2011 Poetry Award.

Some poems from this book were originally included in the collaborative chapbook *The End of Mythology* (Virgogray Press, 2012).

Cover art, "Detached," by Mark S. R. Struzan; cover and interior book design by Diane Kistner (dkistner@futurecycle.org); Congress Serial text and titling

About FutureCycle Press

FutureCycle Press is dedicated to publishing lasting English-language poetry and flash fiction books, chapbooks, and anthologies in both print-on-demand and ebook formats. Founded in 2007 by long-time independent editor/publishers and partners Diane Kistner and Robert S. King, the press incorporated as a nonprofit in 2012. A number of our editors are distinguished poets and authors in their own right, and we have been actively involved in the small press movement going back to the early seventies.

The FutureCycle Poetry Book Prize and honorarium is awarded annually for the best full-length volume of poetry we publish in a calendar year. Introduced in 2013, our Good Works projects are devoted to issues of global significance, with all proceeds donated to a related worthy cause. We are dedicated to giving all authors we publish the care their work deserves, making our catalog of titles the most distinguished it can be, and paying forward any earnings to fund more great books.

We've learned a few things about independent publishing over the years. We've also evolved a unique, resilient publishing model that allows us to focus on vetting and preserving for posterity the most books of exceptional quality without becoming overwhelmed with bookkeeping and mailing, fundraising activities, or taxing editorial and production "bubbles." To find out more about what we are doing, come see us at www.futurecycle.org.

www.ingramcontent.com/pod-product-compliance
Lightning Source LLC
LaVergne TN
LVHW020938090426
835512LV00020B/3414